Ape-men of the
SNOW

John Townsend

Published in association with The Basic Skills Agency

Hodder & Stoughton
A MEMBER OF THE HODDER HEADLINE GROUP

Acknowledgements
Cover artwork: Fred van Deelan
Illustrations: Brian Lee
Photos: pp iv, 8, 23 © René Dahinden/Fortean Picture Library; p 6 © Fortean Picture Library;
p. 3 © The Ronald Grant Archive.

Orders: please contact Bookpoint Ltd, 130 Milton Park, Abingdon, Oxon OX14 4SB.
Telephone: (44) 01235 827720, Fax: (44) 01235 400454. Lines are open from 9.00 – 6.00,
Monday to Saturday, with a 24 hour message answering service. Email address:
orders@bookpoint.co.uk

British Library Cataloguing in Publication Data
A catalogue record for this title is available from The British Library

ISBN 0 340 84866 9

First published 2002
Impression number   10 9 8 7 6 5 4 3 2 1
Year   2007 2006 2005 2004 2003 2002

Typeset by SX Composing DTP, Rayleigh, Essex.
Printed in Great Britain for Hodder & Stoughton Educational, a division of Hodder
Headline Plc, 338 Euston Road, London NW1 3BH by Bath Press Ltd.

Contents

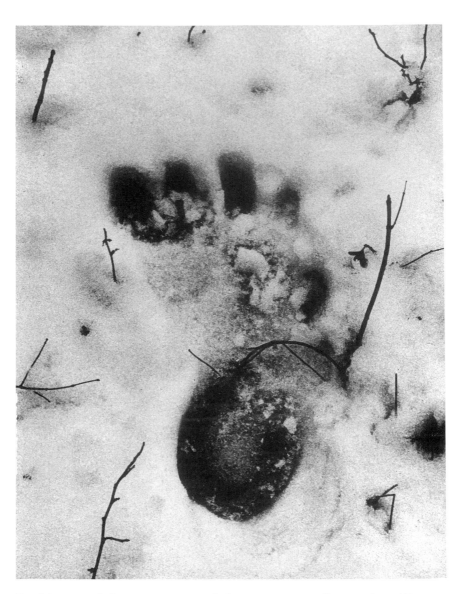

Is this proof that ape-men of the snow are alive and well?

1   Hairy and Scary

Big apes scare us. They always have done.
They were once seen as savage beasts.
But what about today?

Most of us would run if a gorilla got on the bus.
Maybe it's because apes are so like us.
Maybe it's because they are clever . . .
and very hairy.

For years we knew very little about apes.
Travellers told tales of 'great hairy
man-like beasts' in the trees.

It is only in the last hundred years
that we've begun to find out about
the large apes of the world.

No longer are they seen as monsters.
Not often.

Old monster movies used apes
to scare the crowds.
A giant ape on the loose was a box-office winner.
So was an army of them in *Planet of the Apes*.

King Kong first roared on the screen
over seventy years ago.
At the time it was shocking.
It brought back all those
deep, dark fears inside us.

Such films seem very tame now
but they made some people faint!
They hid behind their seats when the
huge ape held the girl in his hairy hand.

An angry ape, bigger than a human,
may seem a bit far-fetched.
But it's only the stuff of horror movies . . .
Or is it?

Old myths from many parts of the world
told of 'hairy snowmen of the forest'.

King Kong – a big ape in a bad mood!

Were these just early horror stories?
Were they just an early form of fiction?

In fact, some say they've seen
these 'ape-men of the snow'
in just the last few years.
Can they still be with us in the 21st Century?
And the question some still ask is:
'*Is there anything to fear?*'
Perhaps truth *can* be stranger than fiction . . .

2   What's All the Fuss?

In most wild places of the world
there are stories.
Stories going back many years.
Stories of shy beasts that walk on two legs.
They are not bears. Not gorillas.
They are the size of humans.
Sometimes bigger.
They move like humans.
But they are hairy all over . . . and they smell.

Some people think these beasts
may be the 'missing link'
between apes and humans.

They could be an extinct early ape-man.
Who knows?
And they don't just live in the snow.
They have been seen in rain forests as well.

Some say there is no truth to these stories.
They say they are just that – stories.
Just like *King Kong* or *Planet of the Apes*.
People have a need to tell tales.
We love a good mystery.
We like to believe in strange things.
We even like a good scare.

But what of the evidence?
Can native peoples thousands of miles apart
make up the same stories?
Can big footprints in the snow
in many countries be a hoax?

Can headlines like, 'Scientists Say
Ape-man Exists' be nonsense?
So why is there no real proof?
We only have a few fuzzy photos.

The only clip of film may be a fake.
Hundreds of treks have gone
in search of 'the ape-man'.
Why has he never been caught?

You may have an open mind.
You may not care.
It may not stay that way . . .

This is how the Ape-man
may look.

3   The Yeti

Secrets lie in the snows
around Mount Everest.
The mountains of Tibet, Nepal
and India stretch for miles.
No one lives in the deep valleys,
the rocky caves and the icy shadows.
Unless you believe the stories.

For this is the land
of the Abominable Snowman.
Local people call it 'Yah-Teh'.
That means 'the beast of the mountains'.
As long ago as 1832,
a British man in Nepal told a story.
He said local hunters were scared.
They spoke of a 'wild man' in the snow.
It had long dark hair.
It had no tail and walked like a man.
And its smell was vile.

Explorers were warned.

The Yeti, as it was called, might attack.

It might even eat humans.

In 1913, some hunters caught

a creature in the mountains.

They took it back to China

where it died a few months later.

It had a black ape's face and long silver hair.

Its hands and feet were more like a man's.

It grunted and made a whistle noise.

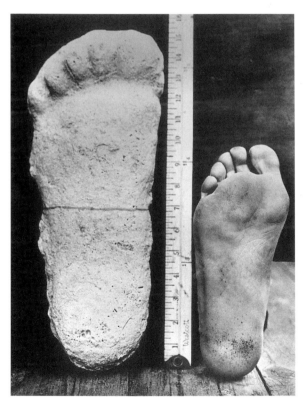

The cast of a Bigfoot footprint next to a man's foot.

Then, people in a remote village
told a strange story.
After working all day in the fields,
the farmers began to go home.
They knew they were being watched.
When it got dark, Yetis came out from the woods.
They began to eat the potatoes in the fields.
They drank water from the tub.
This went on night after night.

Two boys had an idea.
They put beer in the tub.
One evening, they did a bit of acting.
They knew they were being watched.
They had a fight with swords and knives.
Then they fell to the ground
as if they were dead.
They lay very still and waited.
Slowly, the Yetis came.
One by one the Yetis drank the beer.
They got very drunk.
Next they picked up their knives.
They began to copy the boys' fight.
Some even killed each other!
The boys watched it all happen . . . in horror.

The story became yet another
legend of the Himalayas.

Local people told yet more stories.
Villagers in Nepal even told how five people
had been killed by a pack of Yetis.

A girl was looking after her yaks
high in the mountains.
She later told how a large
ape-like beast ran at her.
It waved its hairy black arms.
It grabbed her. It began to drag her away.
All she could do was scream till it let go.
It killed two of her yaks
as it ran off in a rage.

Another story seems even more far-fetched.
A man was lost in the mountains in 1938.
He became snow-blind and dazed.
He fell in the ice and was close to death.
A Yeti came out of the snow.
It was nearly 3 metres tall.
It sat by the man and gently touched him.

It looked after him and
nursed him back to health!

Hundreds of people have gone
looking for a Yeti.
Some said they saw signs.
Others saw nothing at all.

There is even a Yeti Hotel in Nepal
for today's tourists.
The Yeti is big business.
Could that be why people keep telling stories?
Or will a tourist soon have a one-to-one
with a Yeti and get a clear photo . . . or more?

Every so often scientists meet
to study the latest Yeti stories.
Some say they are just crazy.
But many scientists believe the Yeti is real.
They think it still lives in the Himalayas.

In 2001, a Yeti hunter found some more hair.
Experts studied the DNA.
They said it wasn't from a human or an ape.
It wasn't from a bear or any animal
that we know about.
They said it was an utter mystery.
Some said it must have come from a Yeti.

We may never know the truth until
someone tracks down a Yeti once and for all.

In such a vast area in such wild country,
it could take years.
Even with the latest science.
After all, it's a bit like looking for
half a needle in a hundred hay stacks!

Where do you start?
Maybe it's best to start by looking
for one of Yeti's cousins.
For it seems he has
friends in other parts of the world . . .

4 Alma

The Himalayas stretch into the hills
and snowy wastes of China and Russia.
Hundreds of miles from Everest and Nepal
there are more stories.
People talk of Alma.
He is the ape-man of the forests.

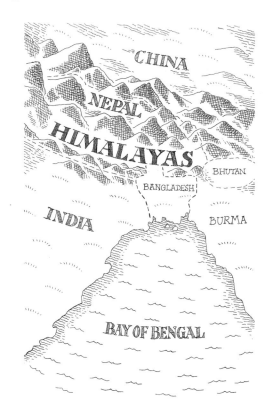

Many argue that our minds
play tricks with us up in the mountains.
People often 'see things' due to lack of oxygen.
This may explain why some people
say they see the ape-man of the snow.

But what about Alma?
He's often been seen in the low lands of Siberia.
Now and again, China says, 'Alma does not exist'.
But every so often scientists change their minds.
In 1997, hundreds of large footprints
were found in Hubei in China.
Experts got to work.
They said two animals
walking on two legs left the prints.
Each print was 36 centimetres long.
The beasts must have weighed over
200 kilograms and been over two metres tall.

Could Alma be a distant cousin to the Yeti
1,500 miles away?
Quite a distant cousin!
But it could have even more distant cousins.
And those big footprints give just a clue.

5 Bigfoot

Big snowy footprints appear in the USA.
They tell more stories.
The legend of Bigfoot
(also known as Sasquatch)
is told in the wild places of North America.
It goes back hundreds of years
to tribes of North-American Indians.
They first told the story of the ape-man.

The Hopi tribe tells of 'the big hairy man'.
He is meant to come to warn them
if they upset the Creator.
Another tribe sces Bigfoot as
an 'elder brother' who
keeps an eye on them.

He appears only now and again –
to eat human flesh.

Many Indian tribes say Bigfoot knows
just when humans go out looking for him.
He chooses when to be seen.
He can escape any hunt.
Indians see all of nature as one family –
with Bigfoot as another member.
They respect him.

Pine forests in Canada are
good places to look for Bigfoot.
They say the sugar in pine needles is
a good food supply in the cold winters.
Unless, of course, they prefer
more meaty dinners.
They are said to like raw meat.
Reports of Bigfoot come from
all across America.
Some say it is brown . . . or black . . .
or grey . . . or white.
Some say they've heard it
calling across the mountains.

A sketch of how Bigfoot may look close up.

There are so many stories in the 'Bigfoot files'.
Here we look at just four.

KIDNAP

One story, from 1924, tells of Albert Ostman.
He was looking for gold in Canada.
He was asleep in his sleeping bag one night.
Suddenly, something picked him up
and carried him away.
A family of big hairy creatures
kept him in their den.
They didn't hurt him, but they wouldn't let him go.
Ostman got one of them to chew
some of his tobacco.
When it was sick, Ostman ran away.
He lived to tell his story.

ATTACK

Ape Canyon is near Mount St. Helens.
Fred Beck and his friends
looked for gold there in 1924.

They once saw many
giant footprints by the river.
Some nights they heard
whistling near their cabin.
Sometimes there were thumping noises –
like a large beast beating its chest.

One night, Fred and his friend
left the cabin to get water.
When they got to the well they saw
a big hairy beast hiding behind a tree.
They were scared and shot at it.
It ran off as they shot again.
At last, they went back to the cabin
and went to bed.
They were woken by
heavy thumping on the walls.
About 20 Bigfoots were attacking the cabin.
They jumped on the roof.
They hit the walls and door.

They threw rocks.
The men inside were terrified.
They shot their guns into the night.

As soon as it was light,
the men crept out of the cabin.
They just had to get away.
As they scrambled over rocks,
a Bigfoot came from the shadows.
It began to follow them.
It looked down at them from a ledge.
Fred grabbed his gun and fired.
He hit it in the chest. It roared and fell.
The men ran and never went back
to Ape Canyon again.

THE HAIRY MONSTER

It was 1977 when Mrs Sites went
into her garden to feed her pet rabbits.
She stood still in shock.
The hutch door was ripped off.
The rabbits lay inside – all crushed to death.

The next night she saw a
large shadow in the garden.
It looked like a man but it had no neck.

She quickly let out the dog.
The beast flung the dog
across the grass and walked off.
The next night, men waited with guns.
Once more the beast came.
The guns fired. There was a roar.
They'd hit it.
The men ran out to look, but it had gone.
A few weeks later Mrs Sites's children
went for a walk in the woods.
They heard a noise behind them.
Suddenly the hairy monster ran at them.
It seemed in pain.
It even held out its arms as if to ask for help.
The children turned and ran.
A search party went back to look in the woods.
But the hairy monster was never seen again.

A BEAST IN THE WOODS

In 2001, some friends in Iowa
went walking in the woods at night.
They saw something 'big and hairy'
hiding behind a bush.

It had huge hands, which held a tree trunk.
They ran off in a mad panic.
They went back the next day
to see if there was any sign of the ape-man.
They found a large bone.
After digging around some more, they found
about 20 more bones and a lot of fur.
They came across a dead deer
with its back bitten to shreds.
Had the friends come across Bigfoot
having his supper?
Was it a bear?
Or was it just another made-up story
to scare the locals?

Such reports raise a lot of questions.
Why are there still no photos
or videos of Bigfoot?
Most people say they are too shocked
and don't have time to get their camera.
Most sightings last for only a few seconds.

In fact, Patterson's clip of film from 1967
is still the only moving image.

Some say it's just a fake.
Many experts say it's real.

In a country with more cameras
than anywhere else on earth,
it can only be a matter of time before
Bigfoot is a film star.
That's if he's really out there.

The famous image from Patterson's 1967
film. (*Photo Patterson/Gimlin © 1968 Dahinden.*)

6 Yowi

Aborigines of Australia told stories
for thousands of years.
They have nothing to do with ape-men of the snow.
They're about an ape-man of the forest.
The legend tells that a savage race of ape-men
lived in the land.
The Aborigines arrived and killed them.
All but a few.
They ran to the woods –
where some still live today.

The Aborigines called it 'youree'.
It means 'hairy man monster'.
Today it is known as The Yowi.
When white men first went to Australia
they didn't believe the legend.
They thought the Aborigines
were trying to scare them away.

But by 1800, many people had seen it.
Some tried to shoot it.
They said it looked like a cross between
a baboon and a man.

People report seeing the Yowi today
all across Australia.
There are many wild areas with thick forests.
The remote mountains in the south-east
have many sightings each year.
A Yowi's eyes are said to shine
red or yellow in the moonlight.
And yes, they also smell.
Some say they are worse than
a skunk fed on rotten eggs!

In 1997, an English woman came
face to face with a Yowi.
She was staying in a hotel on holiday
in the Tanami Desert.

A noise outside her window woke her.
When she looked outside,
she saw a huge hairy ape.

She said it was so ugly and its smell was vile.
It was almost human, with sad, scared eyes.
It made a deep roar and then
a cry like a human baby.
It crashed through a fence
and ran off into the woods.

They say a Yowi will eat anything.
It raids dustbins, picks fruit and
even the odd kangaroo!
In some parts of Australia, people are
warned not to walk alone at night in the bush.
Yowis stay clear of a group of people
but may follow someone on their own.
They've been said to turn nasty at times.

Even so, there are no proper photos.
Proof is thin on the ground.
But there again, so are Yowis!

7   Where Next?

Some like to think we still have
a living ancestor out there.
Some like to think these ape-men really exist.

Others say 'maybe'.
Maybe there is some truth
in a few of these stories.
After all, how is it that
so many places tell such stories?
There are more from Africa, Brazil and Japan.
And all those footprints got there somehow.

Others dismiss the whole subject.
Like King Kong, it's all pure fiction.
It's just people being taken in by a huge hoax.
After all, why has a dead ape-man
never been found?

In fact, no one ever seems to
find any dead ape or bear.
Dead bodies in the wild are soon picked clean.
Sick animals will often take themselves far off
to very remote places to die.
Their bodies are never found.
Nature does the rest.
Yet there are many fossils of what
could have been the ape-man.

New reports and details can be found at:
www.yowiehunters.com
www.forteanpix.demon.co.uk/bigfoot.html
www.sonic.net/~anomaly/articles/ga00001.shtml

It surely won't be long now before the ape-man
of the snow is proved once and for all.
Either as the biggest hoax of all time
or as our rare long-lost cousin.
He may well become part of the family . . .
once he's had a proper bath, of course!